The Human Element

The Human Element

Brianna Wiest

THOUGHT CATALOG BOOKS

Copyright © 2015 by The Thought & Expression Co.

All rights reserved. Published by Thought Catalog Books, a division of The Thought & Expression Co., Williamsburg, Brooklyn.

For general information and submissions: hello@thoughtcatalog.com.

First edition, 2015.

ISBN 978-1515216469

10 9 8 7 6 5 4 3 2 1

Founded in 2010, Thought Catalog is a website and imprint dedicated to your ideas and stories. We publish fiction and non-fiction from emerging and established writers across all genres.

Cover photography by Coley Brown

Dedication

For Jake, the first to prove that the best things would be unexpected.

Contents

	Introduction	1
1.	We Are Coexisting Truths	5
2.	The Choice You Don't Realize You Have	11
3.	Out Of Body And Into Light	18
4.	How To Lose Yourself	24
5.	What Only Exists In Your Mind	32
6.	The Temporary Within The Eternal	36
7.	The Mind May Forget, But The Soul Is Embedded	40
8.	Peace Is Inside The Acceptance Of Temporariness	45

9.	Your Life Unfolds From Your Inner Self, Not Your Inner Mind	*51*
10.	Love As The Catalyst	*56*
11.	Where You Find Your Purpose	*63*
12.	Accepting Who You Are Vs. Accepting What You Are	*68*
13.	The Only Comparison Worth Making	*73*
14.	The Relentless Mind	*77*
15.	Finding Your Own Spiritual Experiences	*81*
16.	The Place From Where You Understand Good And Bad	*89*
17.	The Opposite Of Humanness	*97*
	Acknowledgements	*105*
	About the Author	*107*

Introduction

You do not have to be a deeply spiritual person to understand what the human element is, or how it applies to you, or what you are supposed to do with this book once you read it.

For starters, you have to be a person.

But then again, maybe you don't. I have a feeling that Brianna would say that pets have a human element in them too, which is not to say that this is the kind of book that is lofty and far-reaching and ascribes meaning to even the most mundane things, because it isn't.

What I mean to say is that the human element is in everything, because the meaning is already there. The meaning is the element. The meaning already resides in us, we just have to begin to search for it.

This is where Brianna Wiest comes into play.

For as long as I've read her work – and indeed,

even before then — she's been the kind of person who believes that you already have all the answers. That we all do, that they lie somewhere deep within us, but there is a lot of noise and static and (to use a word that she would actually use, because whatever your image of her, she does swear) bullshit that drowns them all out. We forget how to be human, in part because we go through the motions of life, in part because we have machines and obligations that allow and enable and encourage us to forget, in part because it is easier to forget to be human. When you're not human, you don't have to feel. All you have to do is stopper these things down and keep going. Aimlessly. Toward what, it doesn't really matter, just as long as you keep going.

This is, of course, no way to live, and we know this. But rarely do we listen. Or if we try to, it's hard to snap ourselves out of the framework we've set up, that the world has set up for us, that would be convenient to keep going.

The human element, the thing that resides in all of us and pushes against being constrained and will not be kept down, no matter how hard we try, does not and will not have that kind of life. And so it acts up, and we feel like something is wrong with us, instead of asking the question we need to be asking — why?

INTRODUCTION

Why, is an important question. Why this? Why anything? Why now?

But Brianna does not pretend to know the answers. This is not a self-help book. This is a tool, a key, a code. How to examine yourself, how to question your life and what you're doing with it, how to untap who you truly are, and go from there. She does not have those answers. She knows that. She is understanding and knows a lot that way.

And she knows that you do, too.

We all have our purpose in life. Some of us are meant to understand before other people do, and they are the souls that get it and go on and leave us with promises of what might be for us, too. Other people, however, get it and come back for the souls who are taking a little while longer. Brianna came into my life when I was struggling with how long it was taking me. She grabbed me by the hand, and now I don't think I'll ever let go.

Because some people are supposed to walk through the steps all over again with you. They learn twice. They know we are always learning.

The human element is always hungry for knowledge, for wisdom, for truth.

You will find it, no matter how spiritual or unspiritual you are. You just have to trust a little. But you can do that. It's within you to be able to do that. It always has been.

Ella Ceron
June 24, 2014

1

We Are Coexisting Truths

The most symptomatic challenge we face in our daily lives is trying to mentally bridge the gaps between our coexisting truths.

There are dichotomies between which we exist and fluctuate: the things that unfold that we at once know and yet could not have possibly known. The things we understand without reason, the beliefs we adhere to without question. What logic shows and philosophy counters. What we immediately perceive ourselves to be and the nature in which we actually exist. There is no one truth greater than another, only perceptions more fitted to our awareness at various points in time.

If we are never probed to consider what exists

beneath the physical—how the physical exists because of it—we lose ourselves, ironically, in the idea that the "self" is all there is, and that it—we—are defined by what we do, how we appear, and how other people perceive these things. Ironically, the idea of "self" mostly revolves around other people.

This, above all else, may be the greatest coexisting truth we have to accept. That we at once can be impermanent and yet eternal, a duality in a single form, conscious and yet to different degrees. Conscious *of this* to different degrees.

When we only accept what we can physically perceive to be reality, we spend our time placing meaning on things that are ultimately meaningless and temporary. We remain feeling inadequate by comparison because our only gauge of worth is physical, and therefore, through one another. We define ourselves by titles and labels that are limiting and temporary. We end up pitted against others and more deeply against ourselves. This is what happens when we are too deeply bound to our mind's eye. This is the nature of the psyche, designed for survival. But as a matter of modern course, wherein our physical needs are mostly sustained and survival is not our day-to-day concern, we no longer *need* to function at this level. This transcendence, however, requires a shift toward awareness and to something greater than whatever we are here.

I know. I've had to bridge a few truths myself. I've had this story within me for my entire life. It is the truest truth that I can possibly share, but doing so requires an unprecedented vulnerability, one to which I wasn't too keen on opening up. I had confided my experiences in a few friends, my mother, a college advisor, my doctors, and now a coworker or two, but that was it until now.

I would come to find through other writing, reading and conversation that what I experienced as a kid wasn't abnormal, and the problem was more that we don't talk about these experiences despite how common they are. More importantly, we don't discuss them though in the opinion of many—if not most people who experience them, myself included—they unveil a more pertinent, universal truth, a secret to what we're seeking, an answer to the unanswerable, a pathway to a place of deeper purpose and an unprecedented peacefulness that we are all, at some level, reaching for.

Though I knew this, I still resisted. I just wanted to be what other people saw me as: a student, sister, friend, lover, writer. But of course, we are not the sum of the titles other people use to define us as much as we are not just the compilation of organs and blood and breath that we rest in physically. We are numerous truths existing at the same time. This is not contradiction; this is nature. We exist by paradox, and because of it: nature can only be sustained through a cycle of creation and destruction. Likewise, we are at once a physical self and a metaphysical self, existing as one. The latter is realized through the destruction of the former, or, in some cases, a conscious transcendence.

And such an experience, as I have found, leads us to the realization that we are an inner light enclosed in an outer shell. That the point of the journey is to understand that all things are ecstasy within, but they must be broken to be revealed. Anybody can look back at their lives and see how the things they once perceived to be the most tragic were actually the most crucial. The most valued. The turning points, the miracles, the awakenings. What we all find eventually is that the things we find and discover are not sought outside of us; they are what we reveal, uncover and are reminded of through a specific process that's outside of our control and yet at the same time, suited for our needs perfectly.

The truest freedom is in realizing that your physical self is an illusion. A temporary experience for an eternal being to grow through. You are not the thought; you are what hears the thought. You are not the feeling; you are what is revealed through the feeling.

The concept that we're separate is just another mechanism of the mind. We're at once deeply different, but bound by the same nature. The same as each other, the same as the universe, the same as the maps that show us riverways and paths from a distance much like our wrists show us the same pattern of our veins from close up. Like bare winter tree branches outline the same pattern as our nerve endings. If we can learn to perceive ourselves outside of our human minds, we realize that our own light is a refraction of the whole one, that we are cells of the same body—extensions of each other and yet, at the same time, creations of ourselves. We are the energy of the universe playing itself out for a while. The point of the enclosing is to break through. We can only exist by contrast, in a state of simultaneous creation and destruction, and this is yet another example of that.

Because even when we realize there's an inner self, one that guides us and is at peace, is not concerned with the issues and nuances of the world, is greater than the summation of the parts our minds think we are, there is still something within us that wants to entertain the ego. To stay within the thinking mind. This is the human element. This is what makes the dichotomy a miracle and the final frontier to conquer. We can understand the difference, we can feel it even—but until we transcend the desire to feel socially accepted, universally wanted, superior, external and permanent, we will fall back into those relentless cycles of pursuing just that—but never to an end.

For me, it was a medical experience in which I was awake while asleep, and at once felt the difference between my two essential natures—the light, free, strong, peaceful, beautiful one, and the one it's enclosed in for a while. It was by the very awareness of this that I was able to transform my life—the most salient proof being the fact that you're reading this right now. I find we are often critical of optimism out of fear of it not being true. We scoff at those who have found these truths and who live them, because some part of us is afraid we'll never be able to. But there is no such thing as "too good to be true." There is only good, and there's no other way to live in it than to just fully, consciously be. There is no other way because it is the only truth there is, and it's the ultimate reality that is unveiled when the rest is stripped away.

2

The Choice You Don't Realize You Have

There is no right way to approach a deeper understanding of ourselves; the only thing that's important is identifying that there's something to approach. There are different practices, theories and teachings because these different interpretations and methodologies are necessary for different people at different times, at different points of the journey. Ultimately, the journey is the same, but there are different paths along it, so to speak.

In theory, everything is spiritual experience, we just define them as the isolated incidents in which we become actively, consciously aware of this.

"Spiritual experiences," or "out-of-body

experiences," as I will talk about them, ultimately serve you. Awaken you. Expand your consciousness. Connect you, even just for a moment, with the part of you that doesn't require physical means to make it aware.

To be spiritual is to be human. In concept, it brings awareness to the idea that we are spectacular manifestations of our own energy fields. In practice, it brings awareness to being able to sit and breathe so consciously that your body dissipates from your understanding.

These experiences do not have to be radical and intense. They're not reserved for a select few of us, and they aren't rarities. They are, in my opinion, just moments and experiences that change you by way of making you more aware of your essential nature. They heal you and help you. They connect you with a truth greater than the physical reality you can see and understand. They can be as simple as an intuitive hunch you follow to a positive end or as complex as experiencing your inner self leave your physical body. As easy as sitting and being aware of your breathing, as deep as an hours-long guided meditation. As common as attending a concert, as mysterious as looking at a photo of a certain time period and somehow just knowing you were there. As ordinary as reflecting, reading a book, listening to music, watching the sky, wondering about what influenced an action you took, and what thoughts and actions stem from in an abstract, existential sense.

The point is that each one of these things can remove the veil of mind-centric living, and when that happens, you're commanding from your inner self. The "God" within is the part of you that will not fail and will transcend when your body is done.

The point is not that you can pick up a book or gaze out at a cloud and be changed, but that you can choose to see these things as imbued with truth, mysterious and compelling by their impermanent, illusory nature. It's not that these experiences are reserved only for those who are selected for them; it's a choice. And to that end, beyond the single, isolated experiences, choosing to live from the perspective of the whole you, the light you, is a choice as well.

There's a parable from Plato's *The Republic* that I enjoy, and it goes something like this: there's a group of prisoners chained in a cave, and behind them, there's a small fire. Because of their positioning, the prisoners can see the shadows of moving figures as they carry cutouts of trees and animals and hills. But the prisoners are bound with their backs against the fire, so the shadows are all they can see. It essentially sums up with proposing that if one of the prisoners were to be set free and could see the truth and the source of their fictional "reality," would the other prisoners believe him?

I'm not here to speak to you as though I am the escapee and you are the prisoner. I'm here to speak to you within the reality of what we are, all bound together. Only to tell you that the light is not actually a thing you turn to, it's a thing you begin to recognize in yourself. It's inside, not behind.

The shadows aren't those of other people; they're your own.

You do not have to wait, or rely, on an external truth to explain the reality of things to you. You can choose to shift your awareness, and subsequently, your entire experience, now. You are your own locus of control, if you choose to start acting on it. The problem is that we're not taught how. We're not taught how to live from the perspective of our inner selves. We're taught how to follow the rules, stay ever so slightly in fear, and carry on until we've "done good."

How we choose to look at the ordinary in the context of how it could be extraordinary is what's required to make the shift. It's not that there is one specific line of thinking that's correct, it's that you have a choice of whether or not you want to restructure your mindset on your own terms, cultivate your perspective through doing so, and watch how it changes your life.

The very nature of doing this makes you aware of the mind, and subsequently, of the soul. Of the mind-based and the inner self.

We are conditioned to believe that there is only one reality, and it's the one we can see. It's the one other people can affirm for us, it's the one that doesn't require us trusting ourselves, but rather living on the opinions and convictions of others. No wonder it's such a challenge to listen to our instincts, no wonder the voice within is so small. We've silenced it with logic and ego. Rather, we silenced it with the logic and ego that other people imposed on us.

Here's what we know. We know that we know. We are aware of awareness. We know that our residence here is impermanent, and that in the speck of time between two infinities, we are stationed with reason. Or rather, we can only hope we are. But that hope is rooted in another very real element of the human condition: the need to understand that purpose comes from knowing there is a purpose, and if the observation of our own lives and the lives of others can tell us anything, it's most likely that that purpose is growth.

We're conditioned to otherwise skim the surface of thought and fill each moment with routine and definitiveness. But when we falter from that structure, as we inevitably will—life does not unfold as the mind declares it should, but as the soul directs it—we're met with this anxiety because we haven't looked deeper into the intricacies of daily human life, and the only meaning we've assigned is the one we stumbled upon on the surface. Because the still water after the boil only reveals a meaningless pot, and if we accept this with finality, we'll live within that meaninglessness forever unless we recognize the fire that was beneath it all along.

You choose what matters. You assign value. How that does or doesn't align with other people's collective mindset doesn't matter—this isn't about the ways in which we clash and disagree over subjective takes. This is about what you find when you release yourself from the layers of expectation and preconceived thought. This is not about religion, whether you have it or not. This is about you. This is not theory; this is practice. This is what center you choose to act from, and how it controls and changes your life.

This is what happens when we actualize being the conductors of our own universes and at the same time, specks in the span of a greater one. This is what happens when we accept that this experience is a conglomerate of figments of our imaginations, creations of our intentions, and above all, balances of that which we decide matters. And we do decide. From moment to moment, we decide where our attention rests and what that means, and we structure our own lives like this.

We only ever find what we're looking for. If there's anything I've come to find, it's that for some reason, you were most likely looking for this.

3

Out Of Body And Into Light

The first time I "left" my body, it was involuntary. I was maybe 15.

We are conditioned beings and we want control, chief among many other things. We've been raised by a society (or rather, we're propagators of a society) with a narrow narrative that we're all expected to adopt. Experiences that fall outside of those lines aren't often met with open-minded interest—they're met by fear. And fear was, indeed, the only thing running through me as I was relinquished of physical control, stuck in a twilight sleep state, my two forms in a cosmic tug of war with one another.

I can't recall the first time it happened specifically, but I know that there were at least a dozen or so episodes before I woke up one night, screaming out loud that I didn't want to do it anymore, that I wasn't ready.

I'll tell you the first thing worth knowing about the universe: it listens.

It would happen as I was transitioning in consciousness—falling asleep or waking up, though most often, the former. I'd gently drift out of awareness, though not completely, when I'd find I was unable to move. It was right at that moment, the last bits of knowing before you're asleep, that I would feel myself slip (which is a pretty accurate description for the physical sensation). It was immediately met with panic, and it was as though I could feel every cell vibrating and hear a steady, familiar hum. I would feel it inch up through me, the vibrations and numbness coming in waves. No matter how hard I tried to move or wake myself up, I couldn't stop it.

I visited psychiatrists and neurologists. I was evaluated and monitored. They scanned my brain waves and tried to induce seizures. Every avenue was explored out of protocol, but to no end. I was healthy; I was normal. I was having episodes of sleep paralysis, they called it, a fairly common experience, from what I was told and could infer from their unfazed disposition about it.

To sum it up as briefly as I can: it's when your

brain releases the chemical to put your body to sleep but doesn't release the chemical to put your mind, your consciousness, to sleep at the same time. You're awake in your own body. You're paralyzed but conscious of it. It is surreal and terrifying, the most unnatural experience next to actual death; and at the same time, it is profoundly enlightening. It took me years to bridge the gap between those two truths. That I could at once be this spirit self and still concern myself with the petty, daily happenings my human body dealt with. That I went on living for years without consciously tapping into my inner self, though it collided and swelled and pressed up against my mindset.

The second thing worth knowing about the universe: it whispers until it screams. (The third is that the universe is in you.)

The miracle of it all really had nothing to do with the nature of being both awake and asleep simultaneously, but of what happened when I wasn't bound to my body anymore. It was the first revelation I ever had, though I'm sure I'd heard the message countless times before, it was the first time it registered: we are not our physical forms. We don't die when our bodies do. We go on with all the others that surround us—and go on I did.

Before I delve into what I experienced while

"outside" of my body (I've heard people call it "going astral," but I do not identify with that term), the first and most important part of this experience is that some people write it off as hallucinatory. There are centuries and cultures worth of folklore and theory and stories passed through generations of this very experience, and all the things that people see and hear and do while within it. I acknowledge the mystery and fear. I don't disagree. I can recall specific moments wherein I was dreaming. Those instances were distinguishably hallucinatory, with all the nuanced oddities and strangeness and vividness that remembered dreams often entail. I cannot speak for anybody else's experiences, but for me, there was a distinct difference between that and between being brought to the simple awareness of a self inside a vibrating mass of limbs and organs. It's a difference in perception, and it is distinct.

Even if you fall in the camp of people who stand by their conviction that *all of it* was hallucinatory, I respect that, and I understand. Regardless of whether or not it was me experiencing my own fiction, I have to stand by the fact that such assertions do not matter as much as what I learned and how I was transformed once I finally put the pieces together.

As soon as I reached the crux point of falling into an episode, a few things would happen simultaneously. I would become completely aware of the energy around me. I could sense and understand everything that was present within the radius of the room I was in, and farther if I chose to make myself aware. I distinctly felt the difference between how light and high my spirit body's frequency functioned at, and how low and heavy my physical body was. It almost felt as though the two couldn't coexist, and the reason I was transcending it was for my spirit body to match a different frequency, where it belonged.

I couldn't tell you exactly how long the episodes lasted, only that it felt like hours while I imagine it wasn't actually longer than a few minutes. There are no real concepts of aural or oral communication, so when I say "saw" and "heard," I don't mean literally. My eyes were closed. Most things are a matter of perception even when you're in your body, and when you're out of it, the senses are irrelevant. There's one, overarching sense that is more powerful and profound than all of them combined. It's instinctual and all-knowing. It never fails. (And I eventually learned to connect to it while awake, as we all often do when we "follow our instincts" and "just have a feeling" and whatnot.)

The terrifying part for me was not the dreams and hallucinations. It was the acutely palpable sensation of disassociating your physical body from your other, "real" body. It's the most unnatural experience you can have while alive. It's dying, except you don't go entirely forth into death.

Understanding the difference between my two bodies, and subsequently, the purpose of their joining, changed me. It only took that very small understanding to spark a little flame of curiosity, one of which I would not follow entirely for many years to come. The journey, and the story here, is not an out-of-body experience. That was the beginning. The journey is what I came to understand afterward.

4

How To Lose Yourself

When I was young, I would sometimes sit and stare at my palm and say my name in my head—chant it, almost—as though I was trying to convince myself that this hand belonged to this body and this body was called this name. If I did it for long enough, a surreal but calm sense of transcendence would overcome me. I don't remember how young I was when I began doing it, but for the sake of the story, let's say I was 7 years old. It was the first time I had a "spiritual experience," though I could never put those words to it. It was the first instance in which I looked at anything from the perspective of my inner self, and without being aware of it, experienced exactly how you find transcendence, calm, surreality, and all of those desirable, interesting, compelling things. You remember that the hand and the name that you see and say in your head isn't what's real—what's real is the person hearing you trying to put those pieces together.

It was the beginning of what would become a need to understand who I was, an innocent interest that grew and spanned into a decade-long compulsion. It was a fleeting moment of clarity that at the time seemed like just the opposite. A catalyst and a starting point. Of course, I didn't know it then. I was a kid. I guess we're never aware of the most important beginnings—they only seem like endings, and challenges, and insurmountable questions that have no answers. This is always how it goes, it seems.

I thought that the ultimate understanding of myself would come from finding a universal truth, something that could only be found by accumulating many truths and tying together their commonalities. I've never read anything without importing myself into the story or scene or idea, I've never thought about the past and not wondered what part of the human condition would drive people to act in such ways, and the smaller, lesser instances in my life where I felt that way too. I spent my life learning about myself through other people—through the lens of their experiences. At some level, I knew that whoever I was, was also who they were, though I didn't actualize that knowing.

But doing so was fruitless and left me more lost than I could have ever fathomed a person could be. I was seeking an idea of who I was, an idea that was true and real and sustaining. An idea that would change me and create my life as it unfolded in its truth. And that was something I was never going to find.

The reason I am still so compelled by the notion, and really, the fact, that we are more than our physical beings is because of the belief that I was only the sum of what other people could understand me as that led to my darkest moments. I cannot talk about understanding who you are without having you understand me, and the truest thing I can tell you is that I'm not here to convince you that I'm perfect, only that I've suffered greatly from not understanding who I was, and it wasn't when I understood it mentally that I stopped suffering, but when I started living my life and choosing to view each moment from that perspective that I saved myself.

I do not use the phrase "saved myself" lightly or in jest. I was perpetually falling short of what I was supposed to be. Of what the words and definitions I had used to take stock in myself needed me to align with. I was continually redefining myself in my own mind, really out of needing to find purpose and belonging, out of needing to feel as though I was worthy, and loved, and had a reason to stay alive—out of needing to be conscious of a trajectory for a future. This was the only thing that gave me hope for *any* future. The very reality of being caught in my physical body wasn't something I could cope with, only believing that the pain and shortcoming and failure and humiliation and hatred I felt was all there was. I needed to know who I was so I could have a future. I needed to have a future in mind so I would have a reason to keep going.

If I was a student, I'd become a graduate. If I was an English major, I'd get such and such a job. If I was a lover, I'd become a partner. If I was a daughter, I'd become a friend. If I was a friend, I'd become a confidante.

It's a universal conviction, the desire to know who we are, and it comes from just that: the desire to understand the great unknown looming reality of where the hell we're possibly going. On a smaller scale, in our own lives, and on a much larger one, when we're done with them. Even just the desire for this shows us there's something within us that knows we're more than whatever we're defined as on the surface. That we can call ourselves the names of the jobs we perform, the roles we have in relation to others, our ethnicities, genders, physical traits, countries of origin, but ultimately, that won't encompass the whole truth.

Because what we're really looking for, and what we seldom realize, is that we actually need to lose ourselves. Rather—lose the idea of ourselves. And that notion encompasses and expresses the depth and purpose of exactly what I had experienced. When I sat and stared at my hand trying to piece the parts of the human "me" together, what I experienced when I suffered a breakdown over feeling worthless because I was still thinking I was only as good as other people could perceive me as, and what I experienced when I left my body, only to find that there was nothing to understand about yourself, only to let go of the understanding. Learning to part the seas of your mind and allow that core truth to come to your awareness is what happens. The very act of "finding yourself" has nothing to do with "understanding yourself." It just means being in it. Or rather, relinquishing everything else that leads you to not realizing you already are.

Finding yourself does not mean defining yourself. It's letting go of what you're supposed to be and acting without thinking it through from the perspective of someone else who perceives you as such and such a thing, and only that thing. It's not about knowing ourselves as much as it is experiencing ourselves. The idea of knowing limits you at the end of the day. Once you choose a label, you feel the need to abide by it, sometimes forsaking a truer, deeper truth in lieu of adhering to what should be. You keep yourself and your life within the limits of what the labels and concepts you've conjured up should be, and that ends up controlling how you feel you should behave.

The problem is when the idea of who we are stands in the way of letting us embrace and experience the essence of who we are. Ironically enough, letting go of the conceptual thinking of "self" (being removed from the physical form and thinking of yourself as the immaterial) opens you up to the possibility that you can be more than your mind ever conceived you could be.

We are more than the roles we play for other people. We are more than what we pretend to be for ourselves. We are more than our jobs and who we are in relation to others. We are all of these things combined, and at the same time, those only merge to paint create an illusion that surfaces the truth. Our possibilities need not ever be limited by these terms.

Because losing a job doesn't make you less of a person. Neither does not having a significant other, or a family to be in relation to. Not having a talent you can define yourself with doesn't make you less worthy. You aren't your job. Or your relationship, where you live, where you grew up, what you're passionate about, what you do or what you did or where you're going or where you've been.

You are not defined by the malleable, shifting opinions of other people and the titles and terms they'd use to define you.

We are the intangible but present part from which human dignity derives.

We are what we find when we lose everything we think we should be and stop trying to find something new. We are not what we find in the actions of the past or the potential of the future. Our futures don't depend on what we think we are. We don't only become that which other people can understand. We aren't the sum of what we can prove we are to them. We are not the things we've done or the things we promise we will do. We are not who we think we are, only who we experience ourselves as. We are not our minds or our bodies; we are what experiences our minds and bodies.

We are what we find when we sit and think of every element of our bodies—our bones and blood and beating hearts and breathing lungs—and realize that we are not any of them, nor are we the combination of them. We are not any compilation of the things we physically are or mentally do, even though our minds neatly knit them together to create the person we think we should be.

We are an invisible, inner something that resides there for a while, that the mind that can only understand the bones and blood and hearts and lungs won't ever be able to understand. That we can only experience when we relinquish that very mind. We are the guiding awareness. We are the presence that expands way beyond this one speck of life. We are what we find when we lose ourselves.

5

What Only Exists In Your Mind

There's a difference between what something *is* and what we *think* it is. There's a difference between what we are and what we think we are. Rather, there's a difference between the idea that anything is and the awareness that everything is illusory.

It sounds abstract and impractical, but it's a truth that runs steady through the things that seem to matter most to us: we don't get over someone just because they're gone, we get over them when we get over the illusion that we still have to grieve. We don't wake up one day and start loving ourselves, we start realizing that the reasons we *didn't* were false beliefs illogically held. We compare ourselves to others to craft these ideas, we narrate our lives through the minds of others because the illusion of their perception, when we create it in our minds, is one *we can control.*

And we need to feel that control. When we can affirm (or rather, we can choose to assume and believe) that someone else's perception of reality aligns with ours we find an unprecedented calmness and belonging. We have steady ground on which we can finally rest—we're not crazy, this is real, this does matter. *We matter.*

We create our illusions because we need them.

Imaginary things are easier to see because they don't need to be in front of us for us to believe in them. They always exist. They're always there to comfort us and let us live the lives we imagine we want.

But that's the problem: when the illusion isn't the truth, the two collide eventually. The illusion just limits us.

So the comfort dwindles and discord arises and we find we are anxious and blocked and irrationally upset—we go to war with our illusions. We start destroying the physical because it's easier to kill a man than a ghost. We tear our lives down piece by piece and for a second, we're liberated. We're in the light.

We've let go. We know that nothing matters. For a brief second, we just *are.*

Until the letting go leaves us in the illusion of nothingness. And so we create another one.

The intangible things that are present in our lives are the things we don't think we can go on without. The illusions we have to live with so we can go on with living.

We eventually realize that all things are myriads of expressions of distorted ideas, the simple alignment of the illusions we believe in and how we project them onto the world and into our experiences. That happiness always came from getting the things we thought the illusion would like, and that unhappiness was realizing that receiving them filled the void and then we crafted another illusion to replace it. All false and fleeting things are products of this, and the only way to transcend them is to simply be *aware.*

The past is rosy because the illusion shifted as we did. Our lives are only ever projections of ourselves. Any tension over a given situation immediately dissipates as soon as we look at it from another perspective, because all of a sudden we realize that our perception was just one of them—and we weren't necessarily right.

It's impossible to let go of the things that only exist in your mind. The only thing you can do is be aware that they're there. The only thing you can do is ask the questions, challenge the beliefs, put assumptions and certainties on the table and dismantle them. Question what you were taught. Question the whole and the core and the root and the things that have otherwise gone unquestioned.

The greatest secret of life is realizing that these things aren't part of us. They aren't natural. As easily as we created our illusions we can get rid of them; we just have to be aware that they are just that. *Ideas.*

If you don't, you end up living in the illusion that others have created for you. And you'll call it "reality."

6

The Temporary Within The Eternal

I spent many years trying to escape my body—physically and otherwise. The knowing that it was temporary and fleeting didn't make me cherish it more; it made me want to be released from it sooner. I wanted to go forth and find the light, the greater beyond, the whatever-the-hell that pulled me from the inside out.

At once, I wanted to be rid of my body, and I was too connected to it. I felt wronged and hurt because I was still trapped within my mind's idea of good, bad, right, wrong. I put so much importance and value on that which was temporary and impermanent and fleeting and human that when these things failed me, I wanted to flee them.

I've talked a lot about separation so far. I've posed everything within the context of what happens after you escape, relinquish, crucify the physical body—or at least the idea of the physical body. But there's a crucial element to this that cannot be overlooked—it's not about escape. Ultimately, there is nowhere to escape to. Life and death will cycle on. It's not about leaving this physical body, just transcending it. And I know just the use of that word is yet another platitude, but the reality of it is that we seek to fill every internal void externally, and we'll simply never be able to.

I always believed that life was simply something to survive. I thought that we were here for a time, but that we would ultimately return to some white-light heavenly utopia. I never considered being here a good thing. I never considered the possibility that we don't return to that light state by regulation, but by our energy fielding that result, no matter where we are.

A body is a satellite and a temporary home—an impermanent but safe residence. It can decipher signals and energies and waves and omit them as well. It ensures that even for a second in the span of time, we're not left scattered across the universe. It plants us firmly in matter; it encloses us in it. It forces us to release and transform to transcend. It's the ultimate growth mechanism and the final frontier.

If you choose to think of it this way, cells are like pixels and bodies are like nuclei. We know that we are evolving and shifting and that the sum of our parts is not the summation of us, but we rarely consider the fact that maybe when we're not permanently situated, we diffuse. That maybe we leave shards of our fractured selves on the things we touch and the people we love and the parts of the world that are changed.

We see our bodies as inconvenient, malfunctioning messes that serve only to perform a task or duty that will elicit respect and admiration from others. We live our whole lives on this "body level," only accepting what we see on the surface.

But your body will always fail you, and that's important to recognize. You can still love it and rest safely within it, allow yourself to experience and be changed by it, but ultimately let it go.

Because when your body fails you, as it inevitably will, it doesn't mean that *you* have failed you. When you identify only as your body, you are completely neglecting the sea of depth that lies inches beneath. Your human body is programmed not for transcendence but for survival. If your essential needs are taken care of, you're not going to accept that and stop having "flight or fight" reactions. You'll just begin utilizing those instincts in situations where they don't apply.

The point is that there's no other place worth being than here. It's not something to survive and endure but rather challenge and embrace and field and triumph. It's not something you get through and then move on from, it's something you let go through you and that is what allows you to move forward. Our thinking about it is backwards.

7

The Mind May Forget, But The Soul Is Embedded

One of the core functions of our physical selves, or rather, being attached to the physical self, is realizing there is an unspoken undercurrent that guides and directs us to seek permanence. The need exposes itself in the simple moments of stopping to snap a photo of something, in the letters and notes we save, in our desire for recognition, to pass on an heirloom, to carry on the bloodline. These desires are so innately and deeply human.

There's something beautiful to us about the idea that we'll live on past our time. It's as though we take that which cannot ever possibly be forever and make it so—to have some part of us settle into purpose, and for that purpose to reverberate into the future. We crave the sense of eternity, and we can only apply it to that which we already know. But beauty is one of two things: hope or recognition. Usually both.

Maybe the singular most pressing thing we fail to realize in our everyday lives is that we won't consciously remember the majority of what we experience.

Weeks will wash over to random details that only crop up when prompted, and those weeks will turn into months, and those months turn into years, and we realize that it only takes a day, sometimes just an hour, to be completely detached from whatever seemed so real, so acutely painful, so decidedly unconquerable.

Maybe the most incredible resource we have is our mind's capacity to relinquish these things. This reality eventually dawned on me in pieces, in singular moments, when I realized I could sketch the skeleton of some years, but not the flesh and blood and meat of them. I would try to trace the lineage of a deep-seated fear, and I'd run blank. I'd recognize a random, reoccurring anxiety and find that I had to sit and dig to uncover its origin. It was as though the mind could relinquish, but the soul was imprinted.

I'd have to go back and find these memories, relive them piece by piece, make sense of them from a distance, and solve what it left in me by going back through the motions and undoing what was done. I came to find that the act of undoing was the only thing that really mattered.

Because the memories that remain with us are the ones which our minds didn't have to process. They are the ones we didn't block out of necessity, they are not the ones we had to sift through and make sense of. They are not the ones that have haunted us and so we forced them into remission. They aren't the ones that are so painful they have to be repackaged until we arrive at a safer—albeit not entirely true—new recollection of them. The genuine, raw memories of our lives are the meaningless ones.

It's not about what we remember. It's what lies in what we don't, both from our present lives and the two unknown infinities that rest on either side.

The night I met Steve, I was attending a local venue with my friend to see a band I had never heard of before. She spotted him across the room—her former boss—the owner of an antique shop. He was tall and older but ultimately kind and forthcoming, friendly and chatting with her as I left to get us drinks. His left hand was covered in a skin-colored glove.

I'm not sure how the conversation came to this,

but we ended up talking about how his shop was burned down in a massive fire a few years ago and that he almost died. In fact, a large portion of his body was covered in third-degree burns. His hand, he explained, had been burnt down to the bone. Nothing was left but skeleton. I told him that I was a writer, and that day I had written something about how we don't consciously remember the things that matter most, and that I had used the analogy of a skeleton to describe it. We kept talking.

On the night of the fire, he was sleeping on the floor of his shop. He was on the tail end of an excruciating divorce and was exhausted from the emotional stress—he was asleep shortly after the store closed. He woke up two months later after being in a medically induced coma, only to find out that the firefighters found his body by the door, evidently trying to escape. He remembered nothing of what happened between the time he fell asleep and awoke in the hospital.

But the truth would crop up in sudden, subconscious ways. He'd be sitting with friends by a fire when the pop of the wood would leave him paralyzed against the couch, adrenaline rushing. He'd wake up from dreams in which he'd play out some symbolic version of exactly what happened before the flames engulfed him. He believes that the truths his mind relinquished were imprinted on some deeper part of him, and though he can't actively remember them, he still is in the throes and at the whim of his emotions.

When I talk about the mind's relinquishing of memory, I'm actually talking about two things: that the most real, the most crucial, and the most life-changing realities are the ones that we cannot remember. I am not only referring to what we don't remember within our waking lives, but of course, within the gaping unknowns of where we're from and where we're headed. These answers, of course, we cannot remember for a reason. Not that it's too painful necessarily, but that we aren't yet functioning on that level of receptivity. That, and the fact that even when our minds forget, some deeper part of us remembers.

8

Peace Is Inside The Acceptance Of Temporariness

We exist by paradox, and because of it. If nature were to be in creation infinitely, we would explode, or in the opposite, we would implode. We can only function by the very fundamental nature of loss and gain, a nature that plays itself out so beautifully tragic within our lives; but there is no other way to be, and there's no other way we can be. In a more relatable, honest sense: we know that our lives can never be a sustained sensation of "happiness," not even the most connected and enlightened among us are that way without ever faltering. We are designed this way. We are not supposed to be "happy" all the time, though we deeply abhor any sensation that we perceive to be negative. A bad day becomes a bad life, and we fall to feeling helpless, living at the whim of an internal psyche that was designed to ebb, flow and fluctuate.

One of my favorite Emerson quotes is:

> "Nature is always consistent, though she feigns to contravene her own laws. She keeps her laws, and seems to transcend them. She arms and equips an animal to find its place and living in the earth, and at the same time she arms and equips another animal to destroy it."

Though that example is extreme and obviously relates to a kind of survivalist life that not many of us are actually concerned with anymore, it speaks to the coldest, most uncomfortable truth. That we spend our lives seeking and creating and caring so deeply about our physical accolades, our reputations, our monetary rewards, and we forget that while we are equipped with the tools to create that for ourselves the universe is also equipped to take it away eventually. We live for the sake of creating the illusion, though few of us realize it's illusory, and so when another animal that is armed and equipped to destroy it—said animal usually being nature, time, inevitability—does so, we're destroyed from the outside in.

Chief among the things we seek is acceptance and acknowledgement, and that's why our state of peace and appeasement ebbs and flows as it does. Every last one of us can admit to knowing what it's like to feel the need to please the faceless congregation of people who judge us. We all, at one point or another, have acted for the sake of doing just that—warranting other people's attention and admiration. It stems from a very core reality, and that's threefold: the survivalist mind wanting to be included, the survivalist ego needing to be superior, and somewhere beneath, the mind that's gently connected to the soul, the one that knows it needs love to find peace.

But we can never be fully immersed in safety. We can never go without eliciting the judgment of another. In literal, physical terms, as well as in metaphorical, mental ones, by the nature of the universe, and any given recounting of a period of history, we realize that we aren't safe. Not from natural destruction, not from disease, not from ourselves and not from each other.

On a more literal, modern level, we will never find peace that exists externally. We will never be universally in agreement, and we're not supposed to be—we're scattered at different places on the journey, coming from different perspectives, having experienced different things, having been conditioned different ways.

But despite existing at different levels and stages

of development and seeing these clashing ideologies and frequencies misalign, we forget that they can harmonize. That peace is in the temporary, fleeting safety. It's in the acceptance that nothing is guaranteed, not in an internal war to prove that natural law wrong. That's the problem with the mind and ego: we always think we can prove the inevitable wrong.

I remember one night when I was a little kid, I was sick to my stomach, and as I sat cross-legged on my mom's bed clutching my waist, she nonchalantly said to me: "This too shall pass." I was so young, and she was so unintentional about it, but it was the first time it had ever dawned on me that even the harshest of pain would cease eventually. Not because she said so, but because I knew that it was true—I had experienced that pain before, and I will again, but for now, I had to take comfort in the fact that it wouldn't remain.

That quote, biblical affiliations aside, became my life's mantra. I didn't understand it in the context of a verse or message, only from the words my mother gave me that carried me through many, many years.

But as I recited it to myself throughout those years as a reminder that even the harshest, cruelest pain would pass, I found that it took on another meaning as well: that the beauty and peace of the moment would pass as well. I had the phrase written on different pages of journals and on Post-Its where I could see it—hanging up to catch my eye when maybe, someday, I'd need it. As I saw it repeatedly, even when I wasn't in need of being reminded that pain passes, I realized that whatever I was experiencing now would pass too. That it was all fleeting, not just the moments I didn't want. That there was no other way to save it, to savor it for longer than time and inevitability would allow, to find happiness other than in enjoying what I had for the short time I had it. That the only way to really embrace—to be present in it—was to know that it wasn't forever.

There is no peace to be found outside of us. In fact, pursuing that, or happiness, or acceptance, from anywhere but an internal standpoint isn't worth it. It's not something you find, it's something you uncover in yourself, and you then give it to others. It can only ever come from inside of you, first because that's principle, and second, because the chase will always leave you empty-handed.

The only thing we can know for certain is that we're here for a time, and whatever happens within us is the only thing worth cultivating. We are the only things that span past all the collective moments that inevitably pass. It's the only thing we'll bring with us and the only thing that nature cannot destroy.

9

Your Life Unfolds From Your Inner Self, Not Your Inner Mind

I always knew what would become of me, though at the same time, I was in disbelief when it actually began to. I so often talk about not having wanted to be a writer, and how this career happened for me, or rather, to me, for a purpose other than my own personal art form (that's my belief, anyway). One of my favorite author's favorite quotes is a line by Carlo Levi, and it goes like this: "The future has an ancient heart." Author Cheryl Strayed used the line in a column to express this very idea: that we at once know what will be and yet cannot possibly know what will happen.

It's as though the mind can only perceive what it

sees, but the soul knows otherwise. It's not the "mind" that has its future rooted in ancientness.

One of the most important teachings, and most common teachings, that you'll hear about creating happiness in your life is this: thoughts become things. The fact that what you focus on grows, what you put your energy toward manifests, what you believe in comes to fruition.

What you think about is what you will create in your life.

But it's not so much about what we think, but of what we feel. It's not that we haven't been taught that, but we're still talking about it as though the creations of our lives are rooted in the mind when the mind, by its very nature, is an illusion.

But what the mind can do, however, is cultivate feeling. And when you believe from that core, from the base of your inner self, that's when you start seeing the miracles happen. That's when your life starts becoming what you knew it would. I say so often that I'm most grateful I never got what I thought I deserved. I very rarely add that at the same time, I got exactly what I felt I deserved. The lines between the two are easily blurred, but the reality is that the miracles of our lives are only the ones that we believed in all along, whether or not our minds caught up. The mind does not need to be in the process. The frequency isn't as strong, as powerful, as real, as that of the soul, of the light, of the truth.

But sometimes, for many of us, finding that deep, inner conviction that we're worth more than any one person has ever told us we were is difficult. It's not something you can happen upon, it's something that often requires years of work to remove the blocks to unveil. This is where the work of conscious thought comes in. This is how we cultivate it. It's not so much a matter of where your mind wanders during your day-to-day tasks as much as it is allowing yourself to think out of the confines of normalcy. To start revving your adrenaline thinking about the potential of having whatever your wildest dreams entail.

If you want anything extraordinary in your life, you have to start believing it from your inner self out, and that can only be facilitated by thinking outside of the lines of thought you're accustomed to.

We are conditioned to a very narrow, very particular ideology of "acceptability." We know what's okay, we know what isn't, but what we probably don't take the time to be actively, consciously aware of is the fact that this structural nonsense is just that—nonsense.

The minute you start limiting yourself to only thinking within the parameters of what's acceptable from the perspective of not only your mind, but the minds of other people, you're cycling back through bases already covered, territories already charted, thoughts already articulated, ideas already executed, possibilities are erased. The mind loves control and hates the unknown, a natural dichotomy.

Your mind can either serve you as a catalyst of your manifestations or a hindrance to ensure that you never live them out. This is by the way and virtue of thinking outside of what the mind has already been accustomed to: this makes the mind a match to ignite the fire.

Nothing new, innovative and original will immediately elicit acceptance. As I've said before, people love control and hate change. And here's why that's not your problem: because their approval and whether or not they give it has nothing to do with us and everything to do with them. It has nothing to do with whether what you're doing is acceptable or worthy. It has everything to do with whether or not they are happy and satisfied with their own lives and feel the need to take out their insecurities and shortcomings on belittling others.

Much more importantly: the only part of you that is seeking that is your ego. You cannot function, or create, or live happily from the place of waiting for everybody's approval, as the mind will so often do to you. Because no matter how often we're told to do this, we never actually stop. We never actually listen. We never understand where it's coming from and why, and so we couldn't possibly stop it anyway.

But so often, we dull our shine out of fear. We diminish our brilliance out of not wanting somebody else to judge it. We are afraid to dream out of the box, to act out of the box, to be greater than any one of us ever thought we could be. And the worst thing that the ego will tell you is that it's not realistic to think that way. Because "realistic" only gets you the reality you have now.

Do you think it was ever realistic for any great innovator, writer, artist, engineer or designer who has created something new and culture-shifting and world-changing? It was not. If you don't risk now, can you ever? Why not take bigger risks when there are bigger stakes? What's the worst that can happen? But, more importantly, what's the best that can happen? You'll get everything you ever dreamed of? Why don't you deserve that limitless happiness? You do, you know. And it's not the rest of the world holding you back from that possibility.

It is only, simply, what you think you cannot do. A false narrative, a crippling road to nowhere. Thinking realistically only leaves you with what your reality already is.

10

Love As The Catalyst

The way we subconsciously recognize truth is the way we're taught to consciously recognize love.

The things I've been most compelled by in my life—ideas and people—have never come about by means of logic. No matter what we're taught, when we hear or read or see something that we understand to be more deeply true, we accept it as a matter of course. We are taught that the same should be true of love in the romantic sense—*when you know, you know.* But there are so many elements that have our minds and spirits constructed in ways that make this almost impossible to tap into, let alone understand and trust.

There were only two times in which the recognition of love and truth coincided for me, and those instances were when I read two different short quotes:

> "What is to give light must endure burning." —Viktor Frankl

> "Love fiercely, let it burn everything between you." —from the book of poetry, *I Wrote This For You*

There, in two small notions, exists the most accurate description of love as I've known it—not coincidentally relating back to light in both instances.

I would have to assume that romantic love is the most common catalyst of awakening, in part because we are inherently bound up with it on a spiritual, emotional level and because we are also attached to ideas of expectation and purpose that were cultivated and adopted essentially without our realizing. It is what we often perceive to be the ultimate form of human transcendence, the greatest high we can achieve in a life. When it fails us, we are required to finally step back and reevaluate.

Our minds function constantly at the level of waiting to be saved. It's almost ingrained in our natural psyche—survival means there's an end to the upkeep, there's a light at the end of the fight to keep yourself sustained. It's a modern way to apply what is most inherently true of us: that once, this was merely a game of survival, but our awareness and efforts to put meaning and place understanding within that has led us to the age of reason, and a set of different "evils" because of it. No matter what level we're functioning at, we're doing so with the understanding, or collective consciousness, that there's something to be saved from. And more than anything else, we believe that love can do it, and we wait for it to.

But love can only save us to the extent that it can change us enough to save ourselves.

Our definition of that word is so narrow, we cheat ourselves in that we usually only refer to it within our romantic and familial pursuits. It delves so much deeper. It's our fiber. It is the essence of what we need to become complete. It's what's in the room when someone apologizes for the thing they've grappled with their ego over accepting, when strangers meet and recognize something so foreign but familiar in one another, when someone is moved to tears over the most ordinary of things because all of a sudden, they've found that meaning exists nowhere but, and right now, as I sit here telling you with honesty and knowing that the only love that can save you is the kind of love that is your innermost truth—the core that eventually wins out. Your guiding principle, the thing on which religions are built and wars are fought and life is lived. The remarkable pull each one of us feels to keep moving forward. The infinite part. The thing that's infused in every part of us. The thing that's not reserved exclusively for a person or relationship, but the overarching way of life and guiding undercurrent. Great loves are great for what they give long after they're gone. Not for the egotistical, human desire to keep them forever.

The deepest, truest love you will experience in your life is not the love that lasts forever. It is not the love that warms you and keeps you without condition. It is not the love that is easy and natural and unchallenging. The deepest, truest love you will ever know is the love that radically changes you. When your inner beings come together and by the very nature of their togetherness, the light they refract in and through one another exposes the unhealed parts, the parts you have to mend on your own. The light itself won't fix these things. It can only reveal them. You can't squeeze someone into your brokenness and expect that to make you whole.

The only thing worth knowing about love that exists beneath the surface is that we often find it wielding its deepest conviction at the very bottom of ourselves. The very end of our tolerance, the very destitute place of having every option exhausted. We may or may not realize it, but that's the point. That it serves as the fiber and yet also as the sustenance.

That it is at once everything we are and everything we need to grow into.

Learning to love someone is usually the way we heal those wounds, and it usually happens as we realize we were only ever learning to love ourselves. Love is the most fulfilling of human tasks for that very reason. It takes our sense of purpose and externalizes it—it fills that proverbial space in us by doing so.

And the essence of loving yourself, of course, is an often confused and challenged thing. It gets lost in fear of narcissism, overlooked for being cliché and overused, ignored for being confusing and unclear. But it's very simply being connected to yourself, your deepest self, and then loving someone from that place.

The most miraculous part of my entire life has been love. Though there are many things now that I am awed by and grateful for, this stands apart. Not because I still have it to come home to everyday—I don't. Not because I have someone in my life who loves and supports me unconditionally—they're gone. But because I don't think many people have the privilege of knowing someone who compels you on such a level that you are completely revolutionized.

And I did. I once knew a person with whom I shared a beautiful love, at once filled with sorrow and soul-stoking passion. But we were two people deeply troubled by what life had dealt us prior, and we were defenseless against the palpable intensity of whatever it was that raged between us. We sullied it with expectation and chained it with insecurity and singlehandedly proved that the course of the truest love does not, indeed, run smoothly.

Because the most powerful love, the fated love, the most deeply compelling, requires you to be as wholly yourself as possible. It is the most giving though often the most short-lived. It's the kind that poems and plays and stories and novels and songs are written about. Stories like this. Not about a relationship, but of a whole life that unfolded because you met someone who you loved enough to do that to you. It is the most painful. And that is the point of finding it.

It is the love that creates you, or rather, acquaints you with yourself. Not the pain that ends up a by-product. It's not the love that someone didn't give, it's the love you had to find in yourself, when you realized it wasn't there to give to *them,* though every part of you desperately wanted to.

We end up most grateful not for what we kept, but for what we got in a moment. The truth is that we lose every last thing we love. People are, of course, no exception. Either a moment with them is enough, or nothing will ever be. This isn't about not wanting forever, this is about realizing that the love you find outside of you is the most direct parallel to the love inside. It is about realizing that the people we are compelled by are the ones that we somehow know are part of us, though maybe not physically and realistically for now. The real love is the kind that awakens you to knowing that this moment without a physical means for your internal knowing is not a permanent state, just a moment in time. A passing, temporary moment, one of which you'd have never known you were capable of knowing, had you not known them.

11

Where You Find Your Purpose

I don't believe there are such things as mysteries. I believe that some answers are harder to find than others, that some we simply cannot understand for a time or reason, some our finite brains are incapable of processing regardless—but that doesn't mean they aren't there. Chief among the elusive mysteries we seek is an overarching and yet grounding sense of purpose. Why we're here, and for what. We get so attached to this idea of needing purpose, we seek what's "meant to be," we instantly feel the press and push of something within us grow and rise when we're told, or rather, feel, something is our duty. We want answers. We want purpose.

We place meaning on the things that other people

have placed meaning. There's no other way to grow up and learn. Individual trains of conscious thought have to first be developed by expanding the mind with something, and the division beyond that is what we find if and when those predisposed ideas fail us.

We attach the idea of purpose to some greater, holy meaning. We want to know what our "purpose" is in the context of why are we here and what that does for other people, and in turn, ourselves. We want something to do, we want to know we're not just irrelevant matter floating through and getting by. We want to belong, though of course, our belonging is inherent; anything else is an illusion of the mind.

Whether or not you figure out what your purpose is mentally, that doesn't mean you aren't living it. Sometimes we can't and shouldn't know what we're supposed to be doing; otherwise we wouldn't have done it. If we're on a trajectory, we're going to ride that through whether or not we're aware of where it's headed. And oftentimes, being aware detracts us. Being conscious of what we're supposed to do leads us to do it at the wrong time and in the wrong way.

This, of course, is speaking in the context of purpose being overarching and divine. This speaks to what we want to know is our overall mission for being alive, what we can do to change the world and help other people. But purpose is at once much smaller and much more complex than that.

Your purpose is growth, and your purpose is to be here, and your purpose is to not know what your purpose is and whatever journey you take to find it will be what the purpose of not knowing was. Your purpose is to get up and get a cup of coffee in the morning and happen to accidentally cut someone off and in that 30 seconds that they were delayed, they missed the train they weren't supposed to be on. Your purpose is to read this and to do whatever it is you most instinctively feel compelled to do.

We function at a much deeper, more intricate level than we care to acknowledge most times. We are trying to understand a matter of the soul with the mind, which of course, has its time and place but is ultimately unequipped to do so.

More importantly: the very concept of "purpose" is not rooted in the inner self. The inner self just *is*. It doesn't need reason or justification for being. Just the act of wrapping our heads around some concept of what we're meant to do is limiting and keeps us functioning at a level of the mind—because when we understand what it is we're "meant to do," what we're really talking about is what we perceive other people can understand as what we're meant to do.

A greater extension of feeling as though we have

"purpose" usually becomes feeling as though we have purpose for other people. Rarely, if ever, do we feel that our purpose is for ourselves. (It is, of course, for our own development and growth, but that's another story.) Regardless: there's a great satisfaction to be found in doing things for others.

Of course, this has its faults. Many people do things not out of the goodness of their own hearts, but out of realizing that doing so will make them appear good and loved, and will elicit praise and therefore ego-level love, if not from someone else eventually, then certainly from themselves. The thing about acting on behalf of others is realizing that the part of it that feels good has to do with us, not them. Even in our most genuine pursuits of caring so much for another person that we only want to see them happy, and will sacrifice ourselves for that, there's still an iota, an element, of knowing that what we're doing is the "right" thing, of knowing that if we sacrifice for them, we'll be sacrificed for eventually as well. We can only approach others how we approach ourselves. Others are extensions of us.

The reality of it, and the trick behind it, is that we both have to remain aware of our intentions, and we have to live out our deepest truths and confront our own demons and be brave and fearless and create something spectacular from that defiance and confrontation and bravery. The things that will speak to other people are the things that come genuinely from your innermost being, because these are the things they will recognize and understand as they recognize them in themselves.

When you love yourself and are acting from a place of genuine soul and depth, you will inevitably connect with others. You will naturally help them and what you do with your life will inspire them as well. It's not so much of a decided thing as it is the by-product of helping yourself first.

And it matters because we have to connect, but we can't do it disingenuously. We have to allow our pieces to grow and expand with one another. We have to remove the facades of differentiation, and we do that by helping other people as we would want to be helped. But we can't lose sight of the fact that doing so begins with understanding the self first.

12

Accepting Who You Are Vs. Accepting What You Are

If you think about it, human beings are the only species that has relationships with themselves.

We don't only live to survive, we live to understand our survival. We live to analyze. To craft an image of ourselves that is "acceptable" as we have been conditioned to understand it. To believe that following an outlined trajectory will yield our own contentment and happiness. Just the fact that we can be aware to the degree that we feel that yearning for awakening and lightening and overcoming and joyousness says something. The fact that we absolutely torture ourselves over even the simplest of daily transgressions says even more.

We accept this torture as the human condition, as an unmoving, salient part of our existence. We regard the physical as the only; we have to live with our shortcomings and faults forever. We accept ourselves as *what* we are and not for *who* we are, mostly because we don't care to look beneath the surface.

Even the simple idea of an "us" is created by our minds. It's a fictitious definition from which—and by which—we think we will find love and companionship and meaning and purpose and acceptance. It's also the thing in which we find the most fault because those things do not come from an idea of a self.

When I was in high school, there came a point in which it made me so sick to look at myself, even in little glances, that I took orange construction paper I had left over from a project and covered every mirror in my room with it. I remember it being strange to get up from my bed in the morning and not even evaluate how much my upper thigh jutted into my other one, that the image of myself was completely gone—replaced instead by a sad, orange void.

My appearance seemed the easiest thing to digest—the part of me that was so consumable, so readily available for other people to judge. Of all the things of mine that could be improved upon, it was the thing that was never good enough. And the more

I was attuned to how imperfect it was, the more it drove me insane. Because I couldn't fix it all. And at some level I didn't want to. But that didn't stop the voice of "nobody will ever want you this way. You aren't good enough." And of course, that voice didn't just say that in regard to my physical appearance. Rather, it was an allusion toward the fact that I didn't feel worthy in any other way, so to take the thing that was most easily understandable, was the fastest, most natural thing to relay that frustration.

An admission like this isn't exactly easy or un-embarrassing to make. But I do it, as I do when admitting to all the un-beautiful things about myself, with purpose. I came to believe that getting to a point of being okay with my body was accepting that I had flaws and that that was okay. That I would just have to deal with always being a little insecure.

We tend to accept ourselves as a matter of course. It's what's preached to us all the time: that all of life and happiness and goodness can only begin with accepting ourselves as we are. *As we are.*

When we accept ourselves "as (what) we are," we're overlooking a huge aspect of that overarching statement: there are parts of us that are not really us. There are things we're holding onto, pain we've identified with, labels and titles and issues that are so part of our lives we make ourselves them. We're insecure, we're nervous, we're anxious, we're this and that and the other shitty thing. And then we just not only become "okay" with that, we placate it into existence by doing so.

I learned that I wasn't an insecure person, and that the insecurity wasn't what I had to accept. I didn't have to accept myself as I was, I had to accept myself as I wasn't—when I removed myself from all of the ideas of who I should be.

Or rather, what I really mean by this is: don't accept yourself how you think you are. People often take their resolvable issues, their blocks or whatever, and let them be part of their lives because that's "part of who they are" when it's not. It's what they've come to learn is a part of them, what they've been told is a problem, all the little poisons they've let sink under the skin. But those don't have to be there. You can heal yourself.

All I had to do—and all I eventually did do—was take down the construction paper and stare at myself and realize that I wasn't insecure by virtue of having to accept that I was imperfect and that's something I'd have to live with—but because my subconscious, inner monologue kept telling me that I was unworthy and unlovable and never going to find or achieve anything. That nobody would ever love me. And because I stayed trapped in these beliefs, two things happened: I fought harder than I ever thought I could for what I wanted, but I also blocked out a lot of the joy and happiness along the way. I sought accolades and approval and merit so ardently that I completely missed the fact that receiving those things doesn't make you happier. Being present does. Loving your life and doing what you enjoy on a simple, moment-to-moment basis does.

What I had to do, and what we all have to do, is take the papers off our mirrors and sit and illuminate the part of our subconscious conversation that tells us we aren't enough, we're supposed to be anxious, life is supposed to look some way or another, and even when it's most uncomfortable, sit with that running current of thought until hot tears are streaming down our faces as we realize what we've been chanting to ourselves all along.

All we really have to do is shine a light in the dark closet and realize there aren't any monsters inside. All we really have to do is pull down the orange construction paper and realize that our fears aren't real; they're just stories we tell ourselves.

13

The Only Comparison Worth Making

The easiest way to gauge our worth is by comparing ourselves to others. We seek out the flaws and most fleeting and minuscule of shortcomings and declare ourselves superior. But this mindset is rooted in narrating our lives through the minds and opinions of others, though it seems like the opinions are our own.

We only know how to measure and compare and gauge because of what we have been taught is right and admirable in society. We only know how to make an upward comparison based on what we know will elicit the agreement of the masses, or at least the faceless group of "people" we're so concerned with impressing all the time.

We don't stop to realize that the scale on which we place ourselves simply does not also hold anyone else, that by nature we are one in the same though consciously separated by matter, that we are not only as good as we are better than someone else.

Because the mindset of "superiority" vs. "otherness" is the basis on which wars are fought and humanity is destroyed. As quickly as we can grasp at an upward comparison, we can slip into the mindset of a downward one.

The only real measure of growth is what you get when you compare yourself to yourself. This is the only thing that really matters. This is the only thing we're here for. It doesn't matter if it's tiny and only makes sense to you or if it's enormous and visible to the whole goddamn world. The only thing that will ever matter is that you are better than you once were, and you have the confidence to look back at yourself not with shame or humiliation, but with the understanding that you need the past to compare to the future.

I have been a dozen different people in my life. I have picked and selected so many labels and titles I allowed to sink into my psyche and define me. Without fail, whatever I decided I was, I became. They all ultimately slipped away because they were temporary identities that I did not feel compelled toward as much as I knew other people easily saw me as.

I thought the only reality was the way I used to see myself from the eyes and opinions of others. So by that logic, comparing myself to them was the only way to gauge my actual worth. Seeing how I would stack up next to them in their minds was what mattered. But it was horrendously unhealthy: it both fed off of the insecurities of others and was ultimately disloyal to myself.

The only thing that matters now is that I wasn't who I was, and that I don't use these words and external means to define myself anymore. I don't need to. I can rest firmly in knowing that I am an essence, not a role, and that other people's perceptions of it are extensions of their own realities, the ones they crafted for themselves. And that every last person I compare myself to will also one day have to come to terms with the reality of who they are and aren't, and that they aren't only as good as they can convince themselves they're better than someone else. Because all of this is a mind game, and all of this is an illusion.

You will only believe you are better than another when you believe there's any such concept of "better" or "worse" when it comes to comparing people. You will only get past it when you don't need these petty, subjective declarations to sustain your sense of confidence. And this can only happen when you find something deeper within you, something more worth taking stock in. It's what happens when you become proud of yourself for having grown, and it's the result of staying in your own lane when it comes to versing yourself against others—it's a delusion that you can subscribe to or not. The only person affected by it at the end of the day is you.

14

The Relentless Mind

We're only cruel to each other because we're so cruel to ourselves. We are extensions of each other, and how we relate to those extensions is simply a projection of how we see ourselves.

The very notion that you deserve your own kindness is foreign to many people. They think that keeping themselves in a mindset of assuming they're naturally in the wrong, they are protecting themselves, they are being aware of themselves. They are assuming that the awareness that they must focus on is the one that perpetually keeps them in the wrong. Ironically, that's the only place from which you can actually do something wrong. If you've cultivated your default setting to be "I am inconveniencing someone else," you'll inevitably think the same of other people. It's a relentless, vicious cycle, and it's all mechanisms of the mind.

You aren't beating someone to the chase by hate-talking yourself all the time. You're only limiting the possibilities of what could be. We do this as a defense mechanism. If we can naturally assume what other people will think of us, we're guarded against their impending cruelty because we're already aware. Awareness does indeed combat a lot of things, but not this time.

You, more than anyone else, need to give yourself your kindness. In moments that are as intense as when you're on the verge of breaking down and as simple and routine as getting ready for your day. The verbiage you allow to flow through your little, inner voice throughout the day has a profound impact on you, whether you realize it or not.

Being realistic means being aware of what is, and what isn't, and choosing to be okay with the things that aren't perfect because the idea of what you "should" be is someone else's idea that you're adopting for yourself. "Realistic" is being aware of yourself as a whole person, sometimes not as awesome as something as someone else is, sometimes not living to your potential, sometimes not doing what you "should," but ultimately trying and not doing these things for a reason, a reason that is compelling to you for some other deeper reason.

You aren't becoming delusional by loving yourself. That was always a fear of mine as well. That if I weren't aware of what "other people would say," I would be out of touch with reality, I would be existing only in my subjective, ultimately false and delusional dream world where I am one of those people who isn't self-aware enough to recognize when they are at fault.

But this couldn't be further from the truth.

If you want to believe that reality is whatever "other people say," you will spend the rest of your life at the whim of a very touchy base. You will never find contentment or acceptance because the shifting opinions of others change as they do. Their opinions about you aren't actually about you—they're about them.

The only opinion worth cultivating is your own, and that comes from acknowledging yourself as an "imperfect" human being but ultimately one who is trying their best. You have to give yourself these bits of kindness; nobody else is required to do it for you. Just as believing the negativity will have you convinced you're only worthy of what other people think of your faults and shortcomings, believing in the positive will leave you knowing that you are completely worthy of loving yourself for trying, and for being.

"Being" is all there is to it. The disconnect is training your mind to mimic your soul. When you can tame those demons, you'll find they part the seas of logic and reason and out comes light and honesty and rawness.

The ways in which you are collaterally wounded by other people's inner battles aren't what's important here. It's only that you end your own and get off the field. It starts by simply being kind to yourself and realizing that until you are, you won't even be able to accept other people's sentiments, either.

15

Finding Your Own Spiritual Experiences

I keep bibles.

I know the nontraditional use of that word may make you recoil a little, as any religious concept alluded to outside of the holy, hallowed pretenses we were taught to view them in does. But there's no more accurate or more powerful way to phrase it, and I want to emphasize that point exactly: that you should keep bibles.

The essence of spiritual experience is being acquainted with your humanity, most often in simple, daily ways. Most *powerfully* in simple, daily ways. It's a matter of realizing that the things that aren't mechanical, the things that aren't logical come from elsewhere, even if that elsewhere is the part of us that doesn't function solely for survival. Because of the nature of the source, these things are often the most important in becoming aware of yourself. These things usually come to us—for the lack of better phrasing—in the form of art.

We see this, and we know this, because it's pieces of "art" that change us. It's not the experiences we have; it's what we decide to make of them once they're over. It's the meaning and beauty of being aware of ourselves. It's what we find in the camaraderie of uncanny recognition. Finding what it means to become aware, and to identify the spirituality in our everyday lives, often comes from simply observing what already is; realizing how "art" (in whatever form it comes to us) changes us. Through sentences or brushstrokes we often find answers we need, especially when we don't think we were asking questions in the first place.

Our whole lives involve cultivating and surrounding ourselves with these things, whether we realize it or not. If you want to know the second thing about yourself, look around you. If you want to know the first, figure out why those things are there.

The bibles I keep, typically, are books. Books that have changed me, and though that comes across as just another platitude, I mean it sincerely. There are just some messages that open you up to another truth, show you to yourself, encourage you to change direction, and you do. The books that have done this for me each carry a weight within their pages. Their bindings are wearing thin and I carry them around in case I need to open to a line, or a paragraph or subplot that makes everything make sense in my life. That guides me and changes me. Or, more accurately, it changes how I see what's happening around me.

I still do most of my writing in a room with three big windows. Across from those windows, written on the wall in chalk, there's a list. The first thing it says is this:

> "Everything is energy and that's all there is to it. Match the frequency you want and you cannot help but get that reality. This is not philosophy. This is physics."
> —Einstein

The rest goes: Behold your vocation. Be a person. The future has an ancient heart. This too shall pass. Abandon hope. And so on.

"Behold your vocation," the words engraved above the East entrance of the cathedral in Washington D.C. to where I am, still, deeply compelled. Words that I had looked at frequently over the past five years or so, but only now understand, only now realize that meaning is more important that happiness. "Be a person," part of the sentence I have written repeatedly: meaning all expectations and labels and judgments were mine to give myself. Inherently I am just a person, a fluctuating, changing person. "The future has an ancient heart," a quote of a quote from a book I read voraciously during the first months of my becoming. The knowing that which we cannot possibly know, and the realization of oneself as co-creator of what is and what will be. "This too shall pass," what my mother told me as a child during a particularly rough time. "Abandon hope," a Buddhist teaching, a reminder to stop waiting for tomorrow to save me. And so on.

What these things all have in common is that they each bore a burden for me. They each gave me a sense of breakthrough, a sense of awakening, realization, a weight lifted. They are what I came to know to be true. And they come from the collective knowing of truth. The knowing of truth that came from individual experiences documented in a way that other people could be touched.

This isn't about telling you what list of words I have written on my wall, of course. This is to tell you that these are spiritual experiences by nature—these are the things, as simple as they sound, that have changed and opened me to a greater light, and these are the things I have learned to surround myself with. The art you consume and the day-to-day functions you go out of your way to perform out of the basic necessities for survival say something, if not everything. I think that the way you cultivate these things is how you connect.

I do believe that the pathway to these experiences is twofold: art and experience. Because art is never about telling you a story, it's about presenting the circumstances in which you can look at something else and see yourself. Experience is something you cultivate for the sake of routine, but eventually find that with practice, your whole life becomes an extension of the practice—you start deep-breathing when stressed without having to remind yourself, you think up a line you've read as soon as you feel yourself starting to panic and all of a sudden, you're okay. This is the point of it. So find it. And create it.

Literature is not fine and art is not coveted and life is not savored over forcing yourself to feel that which you simply don't. The lives, the art, the writing we're told to admire is often too elusive, rare and removed for people to be touched by it. There's no time to create and consume that which doesn't touch you. Greatness is encrypted in your interpretation of expression.

Good art is not that which is conceptually unique

and well executed, though those do play roles. It doesn't have to be popular or widely consumed or unanimously loved. It has to awaken consciousness. It has to make sense of an experience, change a perspective, document a reality, contemplate a history. It is what is left when you tear out some dying part of you and lay it before the rest of the world to identify their dying parts as well. It's a step better than your personal best. It's a shade darker than you care to go. It's a reach in the direction of that which seems inevitable anyway.

It is not that which is so complicated its execution is reserved for a distinct, talented few. It is not that which is incomprehensible to the layperson but understood to the richly educated. It is not that which displays an expression declared great by a figure in society causing swaths of people to follow suit in agreement.

I don't think connecting is a matter of adding onto your schedule, only taking time to break through the structure and find that in the silence, in simply sitting, in cultivating that which you love, you find a life that changes and heals you.

Every single time we walk with headphones in and scroll through another feed and flip through the pages of a book we are filling our every silent moment with someone else's thought, with a new and foreign energy. There's nothing inherently wrong with this—music is calming, immersing oneself in the lives and business of others is entertaining, books are informing and can be enlightening. But ultimately, these things are only distractions. They layer on another level of thought and therefore command.

Daily grounding is important. I could rattle off a dozen things I've learned that have significantly altered my life, but they won't be as important as telling you this: you need to take time to sit. By yourself. With nothing around you and nothing going on.

At first it will be uncomfortable. You don't have to shut your eyes because you aren't meditating. You don't need to feel like you need to fight off thoughts. Let them happen. But as you train yourself to simply sit and do nothing for longer and longer periods of time, you will start to see the thoughts and concerns and energies of the things you place in your life slipping away piece by piece. What you are left with is what's important.

Creativity and inspiration do not come from a predetermined structure. Insight and intuition do not, either. Structure serves the ego only. It allows us to remain focused on something that is simply unreal but satisfying because if we follow it to an end, we receive the love and appreciation of others.

Learning to sit is an exercise that alludes to something greater. It strips away the outer and places you face-to-face with the inner. It acquaints you with who you really are, which is a presence and an energy. And the more you sit and focus on solely that, the more you will find that your intuition can easily guide you, the more you can understand yourself without questioning or feeling like you need to fall in the traps of labels and such. This isn't about finding your center; this is about uncovering your center, which is the only work there ever really is to do.

This isn't about having or creating spiritual experiences, it's about realizing the ones that are already happening and that are already there.

16

The Place From Where You Understand Good And Bad

I've always teetered on being romanticized by some final, permanent escape and recluse.

I have never watched somebody die. I've come close—close by seconds. I've always been able to slip away right before it happened. I've been the only one in the room with dying relatives, stiff and on the edge of my chair, waiting to hear the last rattle of air pass through. Waiting to get help, planning to run as soon as I could. I never actualized this fear. I never realized it until I strung together the pattern of dismissing myself before I could see anybody go. I see how clearly and easily I approach the idea of my own death, and yet how deeply I fear the death of others.

It's the mystery of passing. It's the fragility. It's the parting of body and soul, and an empty body is something I find almost offensive. I don't want to love that conglomerate of cells and tissues. I loved whoever resided beneath for those years. The corpse is the ash, the remainder.

Maybe being so acquainted with a vacant body makes the living ones, by contrast, seem that much more present. That much more charged. As with any fear, I came to realize that it had little to do with the dying and everything to do with death. Little to do with the happening and everything to do with what it meant in a broader, existential sense.

There is something present in the room when someone dies. A tangible energy. A tension, an impending lightness.

There is something deeper, denser, present when someone takes their own life.

There's some violent, abhorrent dismissal of consciousness that comes in the decidedly last moments of life.

It levels its most striking conviction when it comes silently.

It was nearing 3 a.m., and we had just left an after-party, exhausted, getting the final train from

Brooklyn back to Manhattan. My friend and I were walking through January snow in our heels and jackets with hems that chasséd at the edges of our dresses, mindlessly to the warmth of the subway station.

It was busy, even for that hour, with the bustling laughter of people, some drunk and some cold and some scandalized by the gossip of their nights. I faced her, glaring peripherally down the dark tunnel. I remember so distinctly our conversation, because it was one that we would look back on and laugh, embarrassed. How simple we were. How naïve we sounded in light of what would unfold in the coming moments and then hours.

The conversation trailed on, light and giddy. I glanced again down the tunnel behind her.

What I remember, for a split second, is thinking: it would be so easy for someone to throw themselves in front of a train, and envisioning just that.

What I remember is that a few minutes later, amid all the screaming and other indecipherable panic, I would yell at her manically: *I knew that was going to happen, I knew that was going to happen, you need to listen to me, please, I knew that was going to happen.*

My conviction rose as my voice lowered, and I

was almost whispering to myself, and then just reciting in my head:

I knew that was going to happen.

While we were laughing and carrying on, in a second between the time I looked back at my friend and then to the tracks, there appeared a very tall Asian woman standing on the tracks in a puffy, light coat and backpack. Her hands were in her pockets, and she stared, blankly, into the lights of the oncoming train. She gazed so lifelessly that it was that moment that stays with me most. The presence of an already empty body. Palpable nothingness.

There were a lot of us on the platform. How interesting it was, and is, how we assumed our individual roles. I still want to spend hours analyzing who reached down, who didn't care, who laughed at her, who called the police, who stood blankly. And what I did, in a moment of honest emergency, without really thinking about it.

I know I screamed and the police heard up the stairs. I know I mindlessly dialed 911 though I know there's no service underground. My thought and reaction was "get help," not "give help," not the imperative of the verb "to help," but to find someone who would help her—and still, I want to know what that means of me.

I imagined having to walk away from the

remnants of a crumpled body, or worse. But I didn't walk away. We didn't go anywhere. Though we could have just turned and walked up the stairs and gotten help and found phone service, I was compelled to remain right where I was, right until the last moments.

I remember my friend's heels facing me as she threw her arms out in an attempt to halt the conductor's attention. But most of all, I remember the first moment we both knew what was about to happen and screamed in unison. I think we were different together from that point on. At this point in humanity, for where we live and what our culture is and isn't, you don't scream in a raw, humanly instinctive panic and not come out on the other end changed by it.

But that wasn't the single striking, horrific, story-worthy part of the night.

Neither was the weird way I knew before I saw.

It was the reaction of some of the people who were standing on the platform. You would think the lowest low I bore witness to that night was the woman who, in the middle of a Saturday night, decided it wasn't worth it to go on, but the people who walked away and went on with their lives, mumbling such things as:

"God, I have to get the fuck out of Brooklyn," laughing and walking away.

"I literally do not have time for this bullshit right now," and stomping off, too.

"I just wanted to eat my pizza and go home," and laughing to another friend and walking in the opposite direction.

I didn't completely realize the fury I had, but I did realize that it was located in the same place where that woman's absence must have taken hold. So vividly I remember staggering up into Union Square and walking through traffic to get into a cab that finally took us home. We drove in silence for 20 minutes up into the Upper West Side. I remember waking up the next morning—or rather, about two hours later—and for a split second feeling at peace. But almost inevitably, a flash to the first second I saw that stranger, that woman, and felt whatever it was that I felt come over me, and I was right back where I was, going through all the motions of what I had just witnessed, that panic and really more than anything, fear. Because that nothingness was familiar, and that desperation was, too.

It's experiences like these that make it so difficult to find peace and purpose in *everything*. We want to place meaning and understanding and be outraged at what we feel is so wrong in the face of what we see is so tragic. But not everybody perceives it that way. These instances are the most challenging to place in a grander perspective, but they may be the most important.

There's freedom in realizing things just inherently are, and that positive, negative, lightness and density are values we assign based on our subjective experience of what we have versus what we want to fill some blank lack of something. It is this lack that we fear. There's no real value, only what we perceive the value to be. But the creation of that concept—that value allows us space—also gives us freedom to build something that we perceive to be either good or better from the destruction of what we knew prior.

The reality of it is that even though the pain some things elicit makes it impossible to feel as though there is no idea of "bad," it really shows us how deeply indebted we are to that idea. We think death is bad because it's unknown. I was outraged at the people in the subway station that didn't express empathy for that woman. But maybe it wasn't about what they weren't able to express. Maybe it had to do with the fact that they were not yet capable of gauging the severity of a situation. Maybe they didn't see it as severe. Maybe it was a defense mechanism. Maybe they had to react that way only so someone like me could see and reconcile her own judgments passed on them.

Even the worst things are rooted in purpose. Even the most confusing have a means to an end. You spend your life one of three ways: laughing off the suffering, subjecting yourself to it, or observing it and evaluating for others to understand as well.

17

The Opposite Of Humanness

One of the most noble and worthwhile things any one of us can do is evaluate our unconsciousness and bring light to what's driving darkness. But to do so, we have to realize we have a choice. We are conditioned, we are programmed, we are imbued with unsorted energy. Until we start to unpack that, unravel what we think is inherent, and question what we think is definite, we will find that it controls our lives. And we call it "fate."

Being human isn't something we define well. Technically, it's the characteristic of being; in other contexts, it's the characteristic of being *good*. It only lightly brushes over the whole, though it says more of us than not: that what we are is consciousness, and that the only awareness we like to acknowledge is the one we're okay with.

We don't allow ourselves our humanness. We move toward the opposite of that—rote, mechanical motions of people who think and feel but rarely simultaneously. We say we're aware, but are we? Are we are of what's happening, or are we aware that we're aware? Are we only interested in the way things are happening *for* us, or are we noting how they're happening in relation *to* us?

We do not break up our lives by years, really. We break them up by segments of ideas, segments that tend to be bound by and created from intermittent, sobering moments of awareness. This is what elicits change. Our perception of existence is subjective, one that we control, though we are taught that we don't. We are living feigned ideas of what is, and the only time we go onto something else is when we do question, when we do realize things can be different. Our lives move by the nature of making the unconscious into awareness. In fact, it's usually only in those moments that we are able to do anything at all to change and evolve and grow.

If you look around the room you're sitting in, you realize it isn't the same room you saw when you first walked in, however long ago. It looked differently. It felt differently. You shifted your perception of it completely subconsciously, and that was the experience you created. The glow of a certain light that was once romantic is now too bright, what was once spacious and new is now tired and normal, though these perceptions don't have to shift negatively, and of course, they vary beyond a general physicality of a room, but you get the point. We all know what it's like to look back on a certain period of time and feel as though we were in another life, because we were.

It's not too often that we consider what changed though. *Why* things seem different now: heavier, harder, lighter, easier. The only time we can really see this at play is when we hit a proverbial rock bottom. When there's no other choice but to change. Anyone who has ever been there can tell you that you don't just hit the ground once. It's not usually a one-time cataclysmic event that awakens and changes you. We don't hit rock bottom, we reach the very ends of the illusions we can sustain. It's not a place you arrive at once and then never again. You keep hitting the ground until you realize where you are.

That turning point always has to be the same. The characteristic that defines our lowest low is not being in the throes of our darkest, seediest days and thoughts, it's being aware of it for the first time. It's calling your parents and saying you need help, it's checking yourself in for treatment, it's when you realize breaking down is more often breaking open and seeing what's lingering beneath. As all things, our darkest hours function in duality, because it's often through them that we see the turn to simple awareness. And that's the point.

We stop seeing the problem with how the theoretical light glows and start seeing that it is light, and that's all it will ever be. It never meant anything more than the belief we assigned to it, though those beliefs were foundations, sounding boards, strings on which our thoughts and moments and actions vibrated and gave us the sound and reverberation of our experiences. They aren't inescapable, but their nature is within our control.

For the approximately five of you who haven't heard or seen or read it, in the commencement address David Foster Wallace gave to Kenyon College in 2005, he opened with a small anecdote about two fish swimming along when they meet an older fish, who says to them: "Morning boys, how's the water?" They pass him and swim on for a bit, and then one young fish says to the other one: "What the hell is water?"

The point being: the most obvious realities are often the ones that are hardest to see, to understand,

and of course, to talk about. The aforementioned is probably one of them.

But the one to which Wallace is referring is the simple fact that we live perfunctory lives in which we rarely stop to realize that we can choose how we think—what we place value and meaning on, and mindset shapes everything, and mindset is a cultivated thing. We choose to think about how we think. We choose to become self-aware. We can either let ourselves be affected by something or question why we are. Dig down beneath. Shift, sift, become. Or not.

When we stop seeing circumstances as responsible for our internal state, all of a sudden, we don't need to control them. Our happiness is not contingent; our peace is inherent. When we meet a block—tension in a relationship, anxiety in our everyday lives—we stop fighting over the symptoms and start addressing the causes. The roots. The roots of which will always lead us back to one thing: ourselves. And ourselves always lead us to a shift.

We don't need suffering to grow. We suffer as a result of the lack of growth.

A lack of growth that usually encompasses only accepting what immediately and unconsciously feels "okay." The truth is that "bad feelings" aren't bad. If you didn't have self-doubt, if you didn't question, if you didn't experience anxiety and sadness and depression and loss and pain, you wouldn't be totally human. It's the opposite of humanness that requires you to extrapolate the moment and put yourself in pain because you were never taught how to think and reassign value for yourself. The suffering of life is healthy. It's not something to ward off, but it's something that should make way for us to bring awareness to what it's rooted in. It's not about not feeling it, it's about feeling through it and learning and growing.

Most things are at once sublime and beautiful. They tend to coexist. There are some beautiful things that are tragic and sad and yet we embrace them, we are open to them, we ride their tides and accept them. And then there are the sad things that elicit in us panic. Convince us we need to change. I myself never stopped suffering. I stopped seeing the suffering as a definitive. I started questioning why. What conditioning led me to feel a certain way. What element of my ego made me act in the manner that I did. It's not that I never worry or infallibly analyze my feelings. It's that, above all else, I try.

Confronting a feeling once you discover the root comes down to sitting with it. Giving it air. It comes down to the simplest thing: let yourself be human. Becoming acquainted with your humanness. Sit with what's not okay, and say it out loud so many times you render it funny and suddenly irrelevant. The things that we hide within hold the most power. The subconscious mind is many times stronger than the conscious one. Reclaim it by approaching it. If being human is consciousness, then the darker, heavier alternative is remaining unaware. And as anybody can tell you, things are always heavier when you hold them inside.

Acknowledgements

First and foremost, a big thank you to the friends, family and coworkers for their patience while I needed to be alone over the last year or so, and for their understanding when I came back to talk through ideas and chapters. Most of all, for every last one of you who rolled your eyes by the end with complete faith that I'd be fine.

For Chris, your dent in the Universe is felt. Thank you for letting me come along for the ride.

For Mink, one of the most talented and patient women I've had the pleasure of knowing and working with. Thank you for your guidance, understanding and friendship.

For Ella, a godsend in so many aspects of my life. Thank you for the days and weeks you came and spent with me while writing. For the feedback, the riffing, the edits and the brunches and drinks

ACKNOWLEDGEMENTS

afterwards. For holding my hand in the taxi that night, for talking me through everyday life, for taking what's good and making it better.

For Ally, my very best friend in this world. Sainthood is not past you at this point. Thank you for willingly living and hanging out with a crazed writer. I think the free WiFi is a pretty good trade. P.S. You were right about the field (I told you I'd write that here).

For my parents, for your patience, WiFi, open-mindedness, honesty and friendship. For being sounding boards alongside mentors and counselors even when I was (and am) being difficult. Also for being badasses in your own respects.

For my sister, as you genuinely inspire me with your complete transcendence of human bullshit.

For everybody I work with each day at TC, thank you for the laughs, the GIFs and entertainment. Can't stop, won't stop.

And for you, thank you for reading, and continuing to come back. I hope you know you do more for me than I can do for you.

About the Author

Brianna Wiest is an American writer, author and essayist. She is currently an Editorial Director at Thought Catalog, where her writing continues to accrue tens of millions of page views, including one of the most read articles of 2013. Her first book, a compilation of her published essays, was a bestseller in its category. She lives in Pennsylvania and works in New York.

CPSIA information can be obtained
at www.ICGtesting.com
Printed in the USA
BVHW032257010120
568341BV00002B/443/P